World Book's Learning Ladders

Nature's Patterns

WORLD BOOK

www.worldbook.com

World Book, Inc.
180 North LaSalle Street
Suite 900
Chicago, Illinois 60601
USA

For information about other World Book publications, visit our website at **www.worldbook.com** or call **1-800-WORLDBK (967-5325).**

For information about sales to schools and libraries, call **1-800-975-3250 (United States); 1-800-837-5365 (Canada).**

The Library of Congress has cataloged an earlier edition of this title as follows:

Nature's patterns.
p. cm. -- (World Book's learning ladders)
Summary: "Introduction to patterns in nature, such as the movement of stars, the lunar cycle, the seasons, and animal migrations. The volume uses simple text, illustrations, and photos. Features include puzzles and games, fun facts, a resource list, and an index" -- Provided by publisher.
Includes index.
ISBN 978-0-7166-7740-6
1. Pattern perception--Juvenile literature. 2. Nature--Juvenile literature. I. World Book, Inc.
BF294.N38 2011
508--dc22
2010026722

World Book's Learning Ladders
This edition
ISBN 978-0-7166-7839-7 (hc.)
ISBN 978-0-7166-7845-8 (set, hc.)

Also available as:
ISBN 978-0-7166-4122-3 (e-book, EPUB3)
ISBN 978-0-7166-2515-5 (e-book, PDF)

Printed in China by Shenzhen Wing King Tong Paper Products Co., Ltd., Shenzhen, Guangdong
8th printing May 2017

Staff
Executive Committee
President: Jim O'Rourke
Vice President and Editor in Chief: Paul A. Kobasa
Vice President, Finance: Donald D. Keller
Vice President, Marketing: Jean Lin
Vice President, International Sales: Maksim Rutenberg
Director, Human Resources: Bev Ecker

Editorial
Director, Digital & Print Content Development: Emily Kline
Editor, Digital & Print Content Development: Kendra Muntz
Writer: Brian Johnson
Manager, Indexing Services: David Pofelski
Manager, Contracts & Compliance (Rights & Permissions): Loranne K. Shields

Digital
Director, Digital Product Development: Erika Meller
Digital Product Manager: Jonathan Wills

Graphics and Design
Senior Art Director: Tom Evans
Coordinator, Design Development and Production: Brenda B. Tropinski

Manufacturing/Pre-Press
Manufacturing Manager: Anne Fritzinger
Proofreader: Nathalie Strassheim

Photographic credits: Cover: © Minden Pictures/SuperStock; WORLD BOOK illustration by Q2A Media; Shutterstock; p3, p4, p5, p9, p15, p16, p17, p18, p21, p22, p26, p27, p29, p30: Shutterstock; p7, 27: NASA; p10, p11, p14: Alamy Images.

Illustrators: WORLD BOOK illustration by Paul Perreault; WORLD BOOK illustration by Q2A Media

What's inside?

This book tells you about the different patterns in nature. Some of nature's patterns can be seen over days, weeks, or months. Some take place over many years.

Day and night

There are many patterns in nature that we can see every day. We can see the pattern of day and night. During the day, the sun moves through the sky. When the sun sets, the day ends and night begins.

At **sunrise**, the sun rises into the sky.

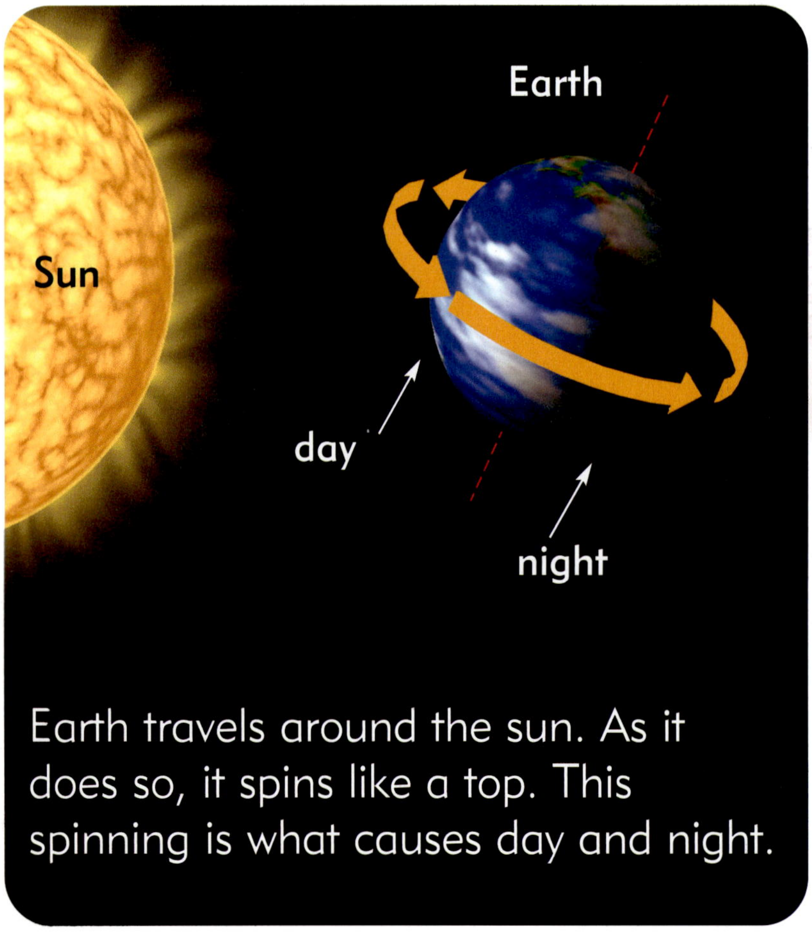

Earth travels around the sun. As it does so, it spins like a top. This spinning is what causes day and night.

It's a fact!

Between September and March, it is nearly always daytime at the South Pole.

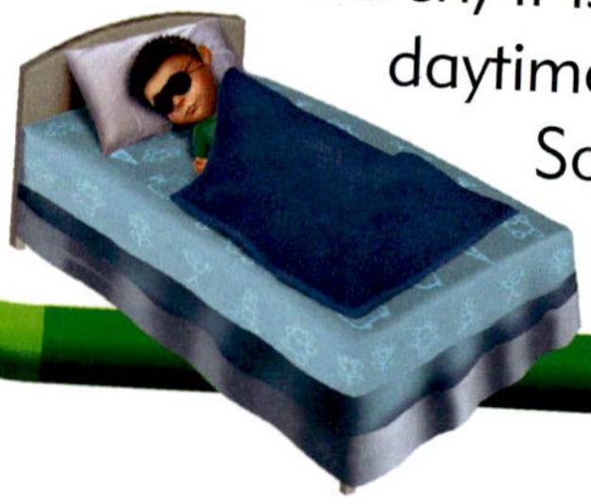

At **midday,** the sun is at its highest point in the sky.

People cast **shadows** in sunlight. The shadows move just like the people.

On cloudy days, the sun is hidden above the clouds. Cloudy days are often cooler because sunlight bounces off the clouds and goes back into space.

At **sunset,** the sun seems to disappear beneath the ground. Daylight has ended.

The moon

The moon is the brightest object in the night sky. It is a huge rock that travels around Earth. Because of this movement, the moon seems to change shape over time. These changing shapes are called the moon's phases.

It's a fact!

If you walked on the moon, you would weigh only about 1/6 as much as you do on Earth. You could jump really high!

As the moon becomes more and more full, it is said to be **waxing.**

A **crescent moon** can be seen a few days after a new moon.

When the moon is completely dark, it is called a **new moon.**

The moon is extremely hot during the day and very cold at night. Astronauts wear space suits that protect them from the heat and the cold.

When the moon is completely full, it is called a **full moon.** A full moon comes about 14 days after a new moon.

As the moon becomes less and less full, it is said to be **waning.**

The moon continues to disappear. Soon

Tides

Tides are the rising and falling of the waters in the ocean. There are low tides and high tides. In most places, the tides come twice a day.

At **high tide,** most of the beach is covered by ocean water.

It's a fact!

In some places, the ocean climbs by 50 feet (15 meters) during high tide. That's as tall as eight grown-ups!

Tide pools are often filled with many sea creatures. When the tide comes in, the animals drift back into the sea.

Stars

Every night, stars seem to move slowly across the sky. Because Earth spins, it looks like the stars move. Stars are huge balls of glowing gas. Stars look like tiny dots of light because they are so far away. But stars are very big. Some of them are 1,000 times bigger than the sun!

A group of stars is called a **constellation.** Drawing lines between the stars in a constellation shows its shape. The constellation shown here is called Leo, or "the Lion."

Some constellations can only be seen during parts of the year. This is because Earth is always moving. In northern parts of the world, Orion appears only during winter.

It's a fact!

There are more stars in the sky than there are grains of sand on all the world's beaches.

Some **stars** are brighter than others. This is because they have different temperatures and they are different sizes. Stars that are closer also appear brighter than those far away.

People can visit special museums called planetariums to learn more about the stars and planets.

Some objects in the sky look like stars, but they are **planets.**

People use **telescopes** to study the sky. Telescopes make faraway objects

What objects do you see in the sky?

Which phase is the moon in?

From sea to sky

Now you know about some of nature's patterns. Can you see the patterns on this moonlit beach?

Words you know

Here are some words that you learned earlier. Say them out loud, then try to find the things in the picture.

stars **tidemark** **full moon**

tide pool **low tide**

Where does ocean life wait for the water to return?

Is the tide high or low?

Which stars are the brightest?

What time of day is it on the other side of Earth?

Season to season

Some of nature's patterns happen over a period of weeks or months. Seasons are the parts of the year called spring, summer, fall, and winter. Each season lasts about three months. Seasons bring changes in temperature, weather, and the length of days. The seasons change as Earth moves around the sun.

Not all parts of Earth have four seasons. In some places, there are rainy seasons and dry seasons. These places have warm temperatures year-round.

It's **summer** in the north when that part of Earth is tilted toward the sun. The days are longer.

It's **spring** in the north when more and more sunlight falls on that part of Earth.

Farmers plant crops in the spring. They harvest them in the summer and fall.

It's **winter** in the north when that part of Earth is tilted away from the sun. The days are shorter.

It's **fall** in the north when less and less sunlight falls on that part of Earth.

It's a fact!

When it's winter and chilly at the top half of the world, it's summer and warm at the bottom half of the world!

Animals on the go

During certain parts of the year, some animals move to a place that has better living conditions. This movement is called migration. Some animals migrate to warmer areas. The big picture shows wildebeests that are migrating to areas with more food and water.

More than 1.5 million **wildebeests** migrate each year!

Wildebeests migrate in **herds** to help protect against hunting animals.

Many kinds of birds migrate during the fall. They spend the winter in a warmer place.

It's a fact!

In the fall, the monarch butterfly migrates from north to south. It crosses almost all of North America in about two months.

Wildebeests live in the **grassy plains** of Africa. They eat grasses of the plains.

Many kinds of whales migrate to parts of the ocean rich with food. They spend the summer eating and storing up fat. In the winter, they travel to warm waters to have babies.

Wildebeests travel during the **dry season.** They move to areas with more rain.

Animal life cycles

A life cycle is the steps that animals go through as they grow, change, and have babies. For a chicken, the life cycle starts with an egg. The life cycle includes all the steps until a chick becomes an adult and lays eggs.

1 A chicken begins life as an **egg**.

Many animal babies are born during spring. It will take many months before this foal (baby horse) reaches adult size.

2 After about three weeks, a **chick** hatches from the egg.

3 A chick is much smaller than an adult chicken. It continues to grow and change.

4 After about three months, the chick has grown into an **adult**.

It's a fact!

Bowhead whales live for more than 200 years! They carry their babies for more than a year.

Forest cycles

Plants in a forest go through their own cycles. Some plants live hundreds or even thousands of years. Others live for only one season. Plants in a forest provide food for many living things.

It's a fact!

The first forests developed about 365 million years ago. That's more than 100 million years before the first dinosaurs roamed Earth!

Plants use energy from **sunshine** to grow. Animals eat plants for energy.

Insects and other living things break down dead trees and other plants.

Squirrels bury **nuts** so they can eat them later. The forgotten nuts may grow into new plants.

Trees grow big and tall over many years. They block much of the sun from reaching the forest floor.

The dead plant matter goes back into the soil. It makes the soil ready for new plants to grow.

Some plants have seeds that are carried by wind. The seeds may float a long way before falling to the ground. There they may grow into new plants.

The water cycle

Earth's water is constantly moving. Water travels from the oceans to the air to the land and back to the oceans again. This movement is called the water cycle.

1

Heat from the sun causes water to become a **gas**. The gas rises into the air.

Rain forests have warm weather and many trees. It rains often in these forests because the leaves of trees give off water. The water rises into the warm air and collects in clouds.

2 Cool air turns the gas into tiny water droplets. The droplets collect and form **clouds**.

3 Water droplets join together. They get bigger and bigger. Then they fall from the clouds as rain, sleet, or snow.

4 **Rain** soaks into the ground. Over time, much of this water flows back to the ocean.

In the woods

Many of nature's cycles are shown in this forest. Which cycles do you see?

Which season is shown here?

Words you know

Here are some words that you learned earlier. Say them out loud, then try to find the things in the picture.

cloud
life cycle
tree
water
spring

What collects in the clouds?

How many animal babies do you see?

Did you know?

The same side of the moon always faces Earth. Until people sent spaceships to the moon, no one had ever seen the far side.

Some of the earliest flowers to bloom in the spring are pasqueflowers *(PASK flow uhrs)*. "Pasque" is another word for Easter.

By studying the position of the sun in the sky, ancient farmers knew when it was time to plant their crops in the spring and harvest them in the fall.

People used to think stars were painted on a great bowl in the sky. Now we know stars are like the sun but very far away.

If a highway stretched to the nearest star, you would have to drive for nearly 50 million years to get there!

Earth has one moon, but some planets have more. Jupiter has more than 60 moons!

Puzzles

Word jumble!

We've taken words from the book and mixed up the letters. Can you unscramble the letters to identify the words?

1. uns
2. rast
3. afll
4. erofst
5. nomo
6. erumms

Double trouble!

These two pictures are not exactly the same. Can you find the five things that are different in picture b?

a

b

Answers on page 32.

Match up!

Match each word on the left with its picture on the right.

1. spring
2. moon
3. winter
4. Earth
5. fall
6. summer

a 

b 

c 

d 

e 

f 

Answers on page 32.

True or false

Can you figure out which of these statements are true? Turn to the page numbers given to help you find the answers.

1

The moon is made of rock.
Go to page 6.

2

A telescope makes faraway objects look closer.
Go to page 11.

3

The bowhead whale can live for more than 200 years.
Go to page 19.

4

The sun travels around Earth.
Go to page 4.

5

Days are shortest in summer.
Go to page 14.

Answers on page 32.

Find out more

Books

The Drop Goes Plop: A First Look at the Water Cycle by Sam Godwin (Picture Window Books, 2005)
This book describes the water cycle, from raindrop to ocean.

Going Home: The Mystery of Animal Migration by Marianna Berkes (Dawn Publications, 2010)
Learn about the migration patterns of 10 different animals through poetry and illustrations.

I Found a Dead Bird: The Kids' Guide to the Cycle of Life by Jan Thornhill (Maple Tree Press, 2006)
This book tells you all about the cycle of life.

Our Seasons by Grace Lin and Ranida McKneally (Charlesbridge, 2006)
Learn about the science behind the seasons. This book answers such questions as what makes the wind, why leaves change color, and why we can see our breath on cold days.

Websites

Hello Earth
http://www.kidsgeo.com/geography-for-kids/0001-hello-earth.php
This overview of Earth has a sidebar from which to choose such topics as Earth's movements, rotation, and revolution; solstices and equinoxes; and time.

Life Cycles
http://www.kidskonnect.com/subject-index/15-science/87-life-cycles.html
From the menu, connect to different websites that explain the life cycles of various plants and animals.

Play Migration Concentration!
http://spaceplace.jpl.nasa.gov/en/kids/poes_tracking/
NASA's website shows how satellites are tracking the many different birds and mammals that migrate.

The Water Cycle
http://www.kidzone.ws/water/
Pictures and brief text explain each stage of the water cycle.

Answers

Puzzles
from pages 28 and 29

Word jumble!
1. sun
2. star
3. fall
4. forest
5. moon
6. summer

Double trouble!
In picture b, the water is farther up the beach, the tide pool is underwater, only two sea shells are visible, only part of the moon is visible, and there is a sailboat.

Match up!
1. f 2. d 3. b
4. e 5. c 6. a

True or false
from page 30

1. true 2. true 3. true
4. false 5. false

Index